INDEPENDENCE DAY

by Robin Nelson

first step nonfiction

Lerner Publications Company · Minneapolis

We **celebrate** Independence
Day every year.

Sunday	Monday	Tuesday	Wednesday	Thursday	Friday	Saturday
	1	2	3	4	5	6
7	8	9	10	11	12	13
14	15	16	17	18	19	20
21	22	23	24	25	26	27
28	29	30	31			

Independence Day is also called the Fourth of July.

Independence Day is the birthday of America.

It is the day we decided to become a free country.

Great Britain ruled our
country over 200 years ago.

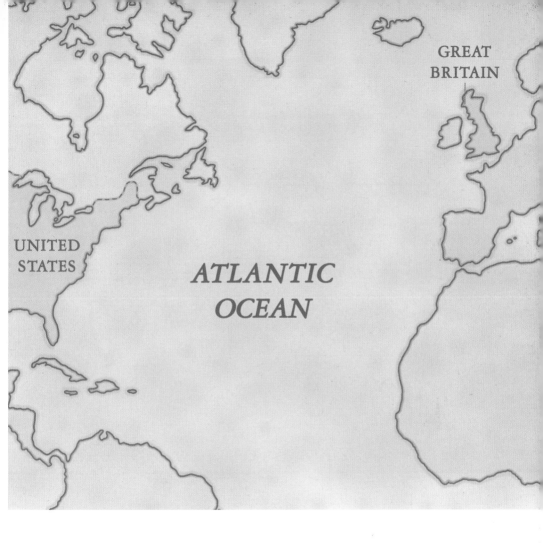

GREAT
BRITAIN

UNITED
STATES

*ATLANTIC
OCEAN*

Great Britain is on the other side of the ocean.

7

People decided Great Britain
should not rule America.

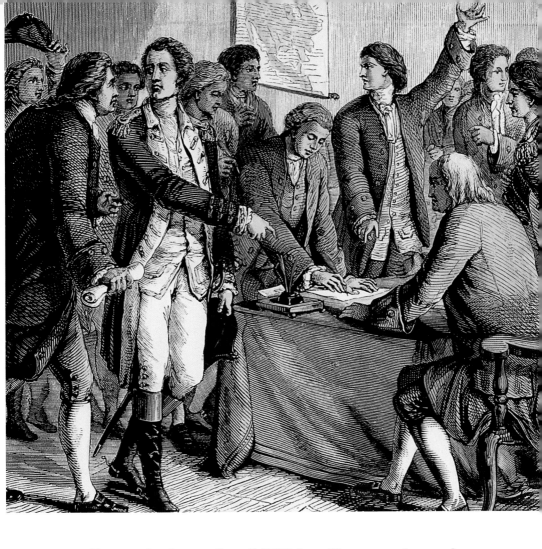

On July 4, 1776, they had
a meeting.

They signed the Declaration of Independence.

It said that America was free
from Great Britain.

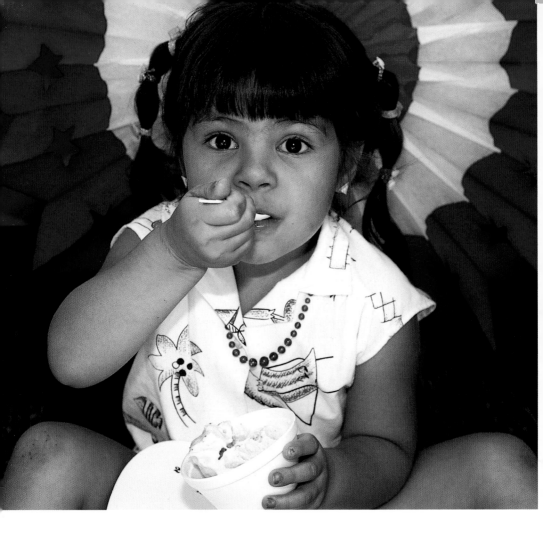

Every year we celebrate our country's birthday.

We **decorate** with red, white, and blue.

There are parades and
picnics.

We watch **fireworks**.

On Independence Day, we
celebrate our **freedom**.

We remember that we are
proud to be Americans.

Independence Day Timeline

1620
Pilgrims from England arrived at Plymouth, Massachusetts, on the *Mayflower*.

July 4, 1776
The Declaration of Independence was signed.

1775
Americans began to fight a war for their freedom. The war was called the American Revolution.

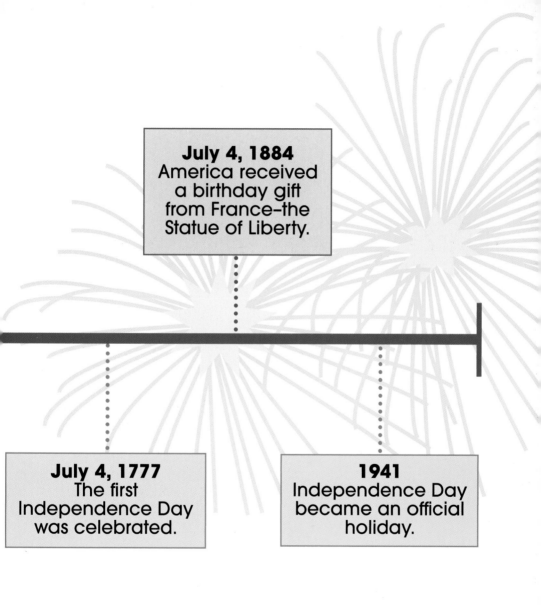

July 4, 1884
America received a birthday gift from France–the Statue of Liberty.

July 4, 1777
The first Independence Day was celebrated.

1941
Independence Day became an official holiday.

Independence Day Facts

Thomas Jefferson wrote the Declaration of Independence. He later became our third president.

John Adams, our second president, and Thomas Jefferson, our third president, both died on July 4, 1826. It was the 50th anniversary of the signing of the Declaration of Independence.

On July 4, 1848, the cornerstone of the George Washington Monument in Washington, D.C., was laid. A copy of the Declaration of Independence is buried underneath it.

On July 4, 1884, the people of France presented a birthday gift to the people of the United States. It was the Statue of Liberty.

Glossary

 celebrate – to have a party or special activity to honor a special occasion

 decorate – to make a place or thing beautiful

 fireworks – explosives used to make light, smoke, and a lot of noise in the sky

 freedom – not being ruled by others

 independence – not being ruled by others

Index

Photos reproduced with the permission of: © Stephen Graham Photography, front cover background, pp. 4, 17; © Howard Ande, front cover overlay, pp. 13, 15, 22 (second from top, middle); © Getty Images, Eye Wire Collection, pp. 2, 22 (second from bottom); © Todd Strand/ Independent Picture Service, p. 3; North Wind Picture Archives, pp. 5, 6, 8, 9, 10, 11, 22 (bottom); Laura Westlund/Independent Picture Service, p. 7; © Buddy Mays/Travel Stock, p. 12; © Betty Crowell, pp. 14, 16, 22 (top).

This book is available in two editions:
Library binding by Lerner Publications Company, a division of Lerner Publishing Group, Inc.
Soft cover by LernerClassroom, an imprint of Lerner Publishing Group, Inc.
241 First Avenue North
Minneapolis, MN 55401 USA

For reading levels and more information, look up this title at www.lernerbooks.com.

Library of Congress Cataloging-in-Publication Data

Nelson, Robin, 1971–
    Independence Day / by Robin Nelson.
        p.   cm. — (First step nonfiction)
    Includes index.
    Summary: A brief introduction to the history of Independence Day and how and why it is celebrated.
        ISBN 978–0–8225–1274–5 (lib. bdg. : alk. paper)
        ISBN 978–0–8225–1318–6 (pbk. : alk. paper)
        ISBN 978–0–8225–8020–1 (eBook)
        1. Fourth of July—Juvenile literature. 2. Fourth of July celebrations—Juvenile literature.
    [1. Fourth of July. 2. Holidays.] I. Title. II. Series.
    E286 .A144 2003
    394.2634—dc21   2001007837

Manufactured in China
7 – SS – 1/1/14